# CLINICAL STUDIES

Poems
by

George
Slobodzian

LIVRES
DC
BOOKS

Cover design by Gerald Luxton.

Designed and typeset in Palatino
by DCAD Enterprises, Montreal.

Printed and bound in Canada by AGMV Marquis.



Dépot légal, Bibliothèque nationale du Québec
and the National Library of Canada, 4th trimester, 2001.

Canadian Cataloguing in Publication Data.

Slobodzian, George, 1962 -
Clinical Studies

ISBN 0-919688-84-5 (bound) - ISBN 0-919688-82-9 (pbk.)

I. Title.

PS8587.L62C65 2001 C811′.6 C2001-900980-1
PR9199.4.S58C65 2001

DC Books, 950 Decarie, Box 662, Montreal, Que., H4L 4V9

# Clinical Studies

# Acknowledgements

Some of the poems in this volume have appeared in the periodicals *Zymergy, Prairie Fire, Prism International, Broke, Matrix,* and *Slingshot,* as well as in the anthology *Sounds New* (Muses' Company, 1992).

The author and publishers gratefully acknowledge the assistance of the Canada Council and of SODEC.

THE CANADA COUNCIL FOR THE ARTS SINCE 1957 | LE CONSEIL DES ARTS DU CANADA DEPUIS 1957

SODEC Québec

# Contents

# Contents

*for my family*

## Clinical Studies

Upstairs    among photographs
so hideous
we were not allowed
to view them
                    (and took
such pleasure turning
neighbourhood stomachs
with)
          lie the single-
and half-breasted women
of medical science
  blinded
by half-inch censor-strips

each with her gown
rolled obediently down
to the waist, incisions
coming along nicely
all these years tucked away
in my father's collection

of human genitalia
eaten beyond recognition

by the horrors
nature concocts
and mankind cures

patiently waiting
for the surgeon
I once dreamt of becoming
to gently put them under
and give them back their eyes.

# Last Thoughts of the Passenger Pigeon — Cincinnati Zoo, 1914

Nobody thinks much
about passenger pigeons
anymore, about the skies
    darkened
in the early evenings
with migrations, the horizon
    by winglight
one vast magnetic thrill
draining North. No,
nobody thinks that much
about passenger pigeons:
monogamous, migratory,
doomed from the start,
soon just another word
for stupid. Instead,

they speak of peace
in the morning paper
that lines my cage
as men sink deep
into their own shit
in the trenches

and I wait to be fed:
crushed seed
for an old bird
gone in the beak.

# Nuca

Let's just resurrect
syllable by syllable

that tower at Babel
and lie naked

on the rooftop tiles,
my fingertips

touching *nuca*[1],
your hands

upon the lexicon,
our bodies

so many stories
beneath us.

---

[1] Spanish, the nape of the neck.

# Art Class

I'm having trouble with the vulva.
Irene tells me to relax, just
let the lines flow as they may
from the end of the pen. I try.
I make a good thigh. Another
good thigh. But as I inch upward
something always goes wrong:
labia lampoon into mollusk;
the clitoris a cowled monk
with angora prayer shawl;
overall, a dark tangle
of briars and disconnected
electrical wires. Frustrated,
I leave it half-finished.
Don't worry, Irene encourages.
Tomorrow we tackle the penis.

## Credo Tropicanum

Spooning papaya uterine rind
onto genital tongue
and holding it there
ripening

down to the very root
of me, made incarnate
if for no other reason
than to eat this flesh

that is never enough
that is enough.

# On the Origin of Invention

Outside the bathhouse window
a spider's web hung
with a dead bee, fishflies
  and condensation
allows the wind
off Koboyama
to circulate with steam
rising from my shoulders
as I lower
with no effort
myself
into the bath, the warmth
surrounding my genitals,
the sound of children
outside laughing.

# Castaway

And so I stood in the wash
pulling things, shaped things
from the sea, things to eat
or merely make my own,
sea-shaped no more:
an earth thing

and the earth took me
for a friend, man-sized,
shaped as a woman at times
because there are none,
brushing and chewing
alongside my own kind
of thing and in time

opening so wide
as to become a constant
swallowing and moving
about my island now,
preferring the inland,
highland to low

yet returning today,
brine-thirsty,
to dig for shellfish

and build
driftwood fires

+

I have drawn approximate maps
with a sharp stick
in the sand
not to know where I am
or how to get there
but to see what it
looks like from the sky

I like to think of the lagoon
as a perfect oval
in my mind opening
funnel-like
into the sea

But I cannot make
a perfect oval

+

Animals I have yet to name
address the meat
I turn on the spit; the wind

sniffs through infinite
species of flora and fauna;
fat drips and hits
the flame: I am not
alone
        In the morning
my bowels say hello
to the familiar tug
of gravity and all
is not so bad

·|· (mammal dream)

I came across a seal
sleeping in the jungle,
black and steaming
in the jungle heat,
sea-contours curved
into the hollow
of a long dead tree,
and placing my hand
upon the curving flank
sensed her dreaming
of the open sea,
green wave-lengths
of light playing
on the jungle floor,

in the black
of her waking eye

+

A man lies in the sun
on a day without end
with an ear for the elemental
radiance—himself

an elemental silence, a man
lying on the beach.

# Pysanka: The Written Egg

In my mind
my grandmother sits
in the kitchen,
drawing the stylus
across the surface
of an Easter egg,
her colossal bulk
shifting as the wind
drives a fine sleet
against the single-paned
window. I am
at her side,
watching heaven
hell and earth
form equal sides
of the same triangle,
the risen sun
a flaming rose
above an endless line.
Her fingers knew these things.
They take my hand.

# Poems for the Dead Guy Who Used to Live here

I

Two dressers on wheels,
a matted blue shag
carpet-clad hide-a-bed,

several yards of blood-
stained tensor bandage,
and an empty armoire:

the landlord tells me
I can keep what I want
and throw the rest away.

II

Eyeing the personal
effects and dust

of Mr. Gerald
E. Moore I must

ask myself why
so many hammers?

Big, little,
wooden, rubber

and metal hammers
in a variety

of designs,
including one

pike-like
primitive-looking

wrought iron one
I gave to her

just because
she liked it.

III

Deceased he still
gets more mail
than I do. Reader's

Digest Sweepstakes
people telling him
he could be

a dead millionaire;
canceled cheques;
timely receipts

and gratitude
from the Cancer
Foundation;

and each month
a TV Guide
I immediately

recycle.

## IV

I had a woman in your room
last night, Mr. Moore.

She was so warm and willing
and smelt so overwhelmingly
of this world I thought

you, who are now no more
than a faint though persistent
bathtub ring, should know.

## Happy Hour

You drank and collected hammers.
That much we know. That you were

a miserable man who died alone
a few blocks from his family

has also been confirmed. The stain
in the floorboards beside my bed

speaks for itself. You don't.
But did. A low voice

seasoned with alcoholic lust
growling obscenities

at passing couples, boyfriends
be damned.... Mr. Moore

may we never meet,
but if we do, may it be

someplace warm, our bodies
somehow revitalized, cold beer

on the table, two happy women
beside us, the men we were

forgotten.

# No More Tears

If you really must know, I'm in the bathtub,
an empty bottle of *Johnson & Johnson* baby shampoo
stuck on my still small erect penis, crying

for help. And it comes in the form of my
entire family, crowding into the bathroom,
pointing and laughing at my predicament,

until my father steps up and turns on
the cold water and I'm momentarily free.

# If I Were Your Papuan Suitor

If I were your Papuan suitor
and you the only daughter
of a rival chieftain
I would gladly risk
my life and honour
to lick the ink
from your blackened teeth
and chew your painted lips
into a long and painful
bleeding kiss
while your mother
shrunk heads
in the kitchen.

And though the others
boast of conquests
in the jungle heat
and missionaries tempt me
with salvation,
I would hold my peace,
your secret blood
on my happy tongue.

# Prayer over Waco

I pray for the souls
rising over Waco

who do not know
the wind the hand the Lord

has sent    his Love
the heat caressing me

carrying me    Sweet Jesus
over miles
                and miles
                        of Texas.

# Calvin

contemplating hell-stench on the shitter
extends a trembling finger
towards his pubic scruff,
inspects for lice, from his navel
picks some fluff.

Then, as if by visitation
from below, a spasm
(not unlike when with his wife)
contracts his lower half
  and posits
yet another statement
of the earthly self.

As the vapours rise,
in insult to heaven,
he doubts not and fears
but the usual amount;
envisioning rather
a celestial ward
far removed
from this wretched world,
the bile, the faeces, and the piss,
where constipated angels
sit and wait for us.

# Suffrage

I cannot help but overhear
the two girls in the seat ahead
answering a questionnaire
in this month's *Cosmopolitan,*
though by nature they are not,
those terms from Latin
fumbling about their mouths
as they both confess
they'll sleep with a stranger
and neither needs a man
with a perfect body.

And listening
it occurs to me
that love must be
a stalwart beast
to haul such crap
and remain intact.

# Fetish

She has returned
from Africa
with a rattle
in the form
of a man,
a nut or small stone
in his empty head.

She has returned
and is showing me
how it works,
its music
in accordance
with each movement,
her arms, her breasts.

## Entering You

is like visiting a country
with no indoor plumbing,
a small corrupt police force,
cultic activity to the South,
exotic cuisine, friendly
though stand-offish natives,
beautiful breathtaking
travel brochure-like vistas,
dangerous water, endless
inaccessible beaches
protected by reportedly
awe-inspiring coral reefs,
a hyperactive night-life,
non-continental breakfasts,
lime-juice
sprayed delicately
over ripe papaya,
raucous primates,
lots of orchids,
too many tourists,
three-hour rainy seasons
every afternoon
followed by amnesia-
inducing rainbows,
and no flights out
until Tuesday.

# Cold Fusion

Why all this talk
about cold fusion
when we achieve it
every other night,
our independent hearts
pumping in the dark
under-insulated flat
for all they're worth
with little else
to keep them going
but the common warmth
we generate for free —
and hope we haven't
reproduced again?

# Letter to Howard Hughes [1]

I thought of you last night,
your money, bottled urine
and Mormons, watching
*Ice Station Zebra* [2]
into the early morning
on the small black and white
I got for my 18th birthday,
wondering what it was
drew you to this movie.

Was it Rock Hudson's
compassionate authority
and genuine concern
for the sailors beneath him?
Or the submarine itself,
its near-silent nuclear
majesty slipping undetected
under thick ice? Or the fact

---

[1] Howard Hughes (1905-1976) — eccentric U.S. tycoon, noted for his extreme paranoia. In later years he retreated into seclusion with a staff of 'trusted' Mormon aides.

[2] *Ice Station Zebra* (U.S. 1968) — one of Hughes' favorite films, in which the crew of a U.S. atomic submarine must retrieve a fallen space capsule at the North Pole before the Soviets do.

nobody could ever trust
anybody else? Or maybe
all the fake snow
blowing comically
all over the place—
a pleasant sight
in Las Vegas
as you sat in your bed
in your wild hair,
your fingernails
beginning to curl
and bedsores ulcerate
no matter how much
money you had.

Tell me Howard,
for I fell asleep
on the couch,
how does it end?

The Russians didn't win
did they? And who,
tell me who,
was the spy?

# Cub Scout's Phone Call Home

### for and from D. O'Leary

They make me wash everyone's dishes, Dad.
Some put ketchup on their eggs, others
Dip mashed potatoes in their peanut butter.
One kid, the biggest one, jumps up and down
Every night naked on his air mattress,
Grabbing his balls and shouting:
*I'm playing the bagpipes, I'm playing*
*The bagpipes.* Other times he beats us.
Please Dad, I've done my best.
Come and get me.

# The Trail

Like a man who wants
to get caught, I leave
samples of my voice
on answering machines
in dark apartments,
little poems
in little magazines,
pubic hairs
in service station
sinks, saliva
on cigarette butts
I didn't smoke,
fingerprints
on stemware
I can't afford
doorknobs
I'll never turn,
and half my DNA
in your mouth.

# Outremont Scene (The Other Man)

I saw your last husband,
children and dog,
walking this morning
to the park, or grocery store
to pick up something,
and thought of your life
with him, the sorry details
you shared with me,
his two-minute forays
into carnality,
your two-month affairs
with his friends,
his passion for stamp
and wine collecting,
your junkets to London
alone. He looked well,
the children happy,
the dog recently groomed,
and I felt for a second
like crossing the street
to introduce myself,
say hello to the kids,
see if they remember me,
the dog my smell,
and maybe go for a coffee,

all of us, on me,
and talk about you.

## Performing Radical

Performing radical
emergency surgery
with a Swiss Army
knife in the back

row of the *Cinéma*
*l'Amour* while watching
reruns of our orgasms
I come across a third

testicle embedded
back of my brain
and gingerly remove it
with the corkscrew

the screen immediately
going blank and all
the golden masturbators
rising to see

who the asshole is
went and fucked up
the picture.

## Her Conversion

When she knelt in retreat
and prayed for vocation
Christ crawled down her spine
and entered her womb

and she returned to the world
and was with child, repeatedly,
maintaining each time God
had planted the seed

at my father's expense;
her body clenching
and refusing to yield
as her last son descended

knowing she had known
the Holy Ghost
for the last time.
And His absence grew

within her, seizing her
in her darkened room
where each night she waited
for one final act

of creation to come.

# Her Interment

The day we buried her
the holy water
froze
        and rattled

off the casket.
We stood between
the headstones, backs

to the windchill,
listening to the bishop,
insulated in layers

of charity luncheons,
hurrying through
the prayers; the creak

of the graveyard
mechanism; her body
acquiring, degree

by slow degree,
its new
ungodly temperature.

## To Her, in Confinement

**"Drive your cart and your plow
over the bones of the dead."**

Out in
what will become
the garden, digging

tearing up sod, shaking
the underside, slicing in
once again with the spade

uprooting as I go all manner
of worms, and worm-like creations,
my thoughts turning, this second

Sunday in May, to you
who at sixty-three threatened
to bear one more child

and died. *So far, mom,*
*we've agreed on tomatoes,*
*tomatoes and snow-peas*
*and something that smells good*
*to climb the back fence*

the trash in the alley
always so busy
with flies.

# Poem

This morning
    a morning glory,
  open, defiant,
trumpeting love
  from the end
      of a pathetic,
 almost leafless
    stem
rising out of
    the dry,
neglected pot
    in which
I had planted none.

# Poem for My Father's Wedding

Observe the old bull
in his winter meadow,
balls hanging low and blue.

The weather he has known
would make a young man shrivel,
send me bleating home.

Yet if ice were to form
across that broad back
that ferried me each summer

safely across the pool,
he would not waver.
In his heart

he is thinking
of spring.

## Prayer for Zoë

Our lady of excrement,
of multiple comings
and goings, generation
and decay, perpetual
motion, wholly cloacal,
mother and father of slime,
the glistening slime

rimming the fetal pool
of broken water
and placental fluids,
keeper and releaser
of pain and all
nutrition, transformer
of death: O spectre

and stench of genesis,
watch over our daughter
now, in the moments
of her birth.

## Translucence

She lies where the sun forms
a small yellow square
on the carpet, struggling
to turn herself over, heaving
her weight onto its side
and balancing there
before falling back
to her former perspective,
her skull in the sunlight
an unopened rose
awaiting further instruction.

# Zoë at Noon

The human form divine sucks
a mango stone, the nectar
streaming down
                                        chin    belly    bum

pooling on the floor
as *drosophila*
drowsily repeats itself

beneath the high chair:
a genetics experiment
brought home for the weekend

by an older brother
the smell of ether
collecting and collating

each generation altered
in some small
significant way

the twitch of each wing
awakening

# Plenitude

Breaking wind and bringing up
a sort of human cheese
she turns eyes
that have yet to determine
their true colour
to the window
uncrossing and focusing
on a point
somewhere beyond
the buildings
other people live in
bring their infants home to
and once every year or so
are carried out of
by ambulance attendants
and moves the sweet curds
about her mouth
with a small pointed tongue.

# Pox

Watching the scabs form
over 231 pustules
adorning her body now

a missing persons map
tacked to the wall
in some non-existent

police precinct,
each inflammation
an abduction

or wandering-off,
a new constellation
igniting her vulva

up around her buttocks
and back    *look papa!*

## Porpoise and Seal

I came home
to my loved ones
buoyantly singing
no man's song
in the tub. Belly

to belly, crevice
to cleft, they
had descended
the aquiline
and were calling me

to join them.

# Elephant Song

and at times
one looks like
an elephant
might look

turning slowly
with his trunk
the new bones
of the dead

as elephants do

not for food
or water,
nor warmth

they just do

# Woodlawn Excursion

I took my child to the cemetery
to show her to the dead
but the dead were nowhere

to be found. We looked
everywhere, overturning
headstones, uprooting

caskets, opening lids,
but no dead. Only bones
held together by clothes

nobody would ever wear again
and bad meat. All afternoon
spent analyzing worm excrement,

measuring the enormous trees
that grow so well there,
setting off small seismic

devices and listening
closely for meaningful
silences, asking God

for a sign, improvising

a turn-of-the-century
séance over an uncle's dust,

constructing an elaborate candelabra
from some of the aforementioned
bones to take home

as a functional souvenir,
recreating certain pertinent
Greek and pre-Greek rites,

invoking the indigenous
spirits seen lurking
beside the tracks

with nothing to do, and
finally, by failing light,
confronting the unknown

naked and afraid. But still
no dead. So I changed her
on my mother's grave and left.

## Poem for K.

**"And I thought of the albatross."**
**—D.H. Lawrence**

You, your entire
wingspan
wrapped around me,

are my albatross.
All night
I shoot ambiguous

arrows upward;
all night
you come tumbling

down. Together,
surrounded
by water, we are dying

of thirst, and something
is beginning
to smell. Keep

your distance.
Never leave me.

# *À la Recherche du Temps Perdu*

To be reading Proust
to you again
in bed on a Friday
afternoon and never
finishing a sentence;
or driving a lost
High Sierra highway,
watching a cow
watching the sun
go down forever;
or landing
a perfect lob
behind you just
to hear you swear
in French some more;
or simply kneeling
on your famous
living-room carpet,
trying to light a fire
and succeeding.

# Graft

They're growing skin
in the desert. Human skin.
From the foreskins

of newborn men. Quietly,
men and women in white smocks
tend the tranquil vats

as each develops
into a small
unblemished square.

Soon, they'll have enough
and a vast pink quilt
stitched lovingly

and spread gently
out over the frozen prairie
to the horizon

self-multiplying
in every direction.

# *Manoir l'Âge d'Or*

**"Nothing beside remains. Round the decay
Of that colossal wreck..."**

Our next stop Sciatica,
to where the emperors
would retire. To your right
the unguent basin, carved
out of solid excrement. Note
the finely detailed inlay
depicting the mortal Hernia
offering a solitary gall-stone
to the muse Hemorrhoida
who can be identified
by her ever-present mastiff
and golden speculum.
To your left, a fine example
of the early fresco style,
with the young Polyp having
his freshly circumcised glans
cauterized at the hands
of the old crone Arthritis.
Descending the stairs
the ornate grotto where
much wheeling and dealing
would occur, the marble floor

still bearing the stains
where the most powerful stood,
awaiting petitioners.
Of course, no visit is complete
without having taken in
the astringent baths, in which,
it is rumoured, the aging
Flatus met his end, choking
on his own dead skin.
In the classical period,
write the historians, poets
would gather poolside
to recite from recent works
for the amusement
of simmering patrons,
periodically skimming
the surface of scabs
and detritus
with long, porous ladles.

# Cud

Had a poem for breakfast
this morning, plain,
unsalted, without exegesis,
on brown unbuttered toast.

Ate it all and washed it down
with 100% Florida orange juice
and walked out, well-fortified,
onto the unreconstituted earth.

It wasn't until later, around noon,
that it began repeating on me —

moist assonance, aftertaste
of half-digested image,
stomach acid, coming up
   unexpectedly
in the face of a co-worker,

iambic flatulence
in the elevator
going down
to street level

and this
persistent fragment
lodged in the socket
a wisdom tooth
once filled.

# Sustain

I want to put
my finger
in your asshole

again, only
with a little more
lubrication.

I want to hear
you make
that noise again,

but with
some added
amplification.

I want to keep
returning
to the instant

just before
the instant
that you came.

I want sustain.

# The Squirrel

The squirrel caught
outside her window
at the extreme end
of a difficult winter
with its nuts down
is a poetic truth
gnawing through

the three-month old
*Glad* garbage bag
on the back balcony
seeking whatever
it takes to make it
to the ecstatic
coitions of spring.

# Extreme Unction

Left alone the adult male
masturbates and writes,
writes and masturbates
until the two become one

unctuous activity,
an unmanageable mass
of jism and ink
morphing on the floor

into whatever forms
he has desired most,
or not enough, and lost.
Thus Shakespeare's muse

knelt a spell
upon his boots,
and Mr. William
Butler Yeats

watched Maude and all
of history perform
a salty, semi-rancid dance
before sliding down the drain.

And so I watch you rise again
out of the self-same spawn.
Take a place beside me here.
Sing me the lovers' song.

# Nativity 2000

Unscrew the light bulbs
burn the tree
return the presents
to the factory

*O let the lord*
*of misrule rule*

Hold the hymnbook
upside down
sing a backwards
Xmas song

*O let the lord*
*of misrule rule*

Quarantine Santa
with St. Nick
turn a reindeer
on the spit

*O let the lord*
*of misrule rule*

Send poor Mary
to the homeless shelter
give her a pill
the morning after

*O let the lord*
*of misrule rule*

But toast the cuckold
and his wife
and bless all bastard
sons of light

*O let the lord*
*of misrule rule*

The son of a doctor and a nurse, George Slobodzian was born in 1962 in Saskatchewan. His poetry and prose have appeared in publications across Canada. He currently lives in Montreal, Quebec, where he teaches literature at Dawson College.

*Clinical Studies* is his first book-length collection of poetry.

AGMV Marquis
MEMBRE DE SCABRINI MEDIA
Québec, Canada
2002